DATE DUE			

3003400080009R

573.7
LLE

Llewellyn, Claire.

Bones

ARLENE WELCH ELEMENTARY SCHOOL

Bones

Claire Llewellyn

A+

First published in 2004 by Hodder Wayland,
an imprint of Hodder Children's Books,
338 Euston Road, London NW1 3BH
This edition published under license from Hodder Wayland. All rights reserved.

Language consultant: Andrew Burrell
Subject consultant: Carol Ballard
Design: Perry Tate Design
Picture research: Glass Onion Pictures

Published in the United States by Smart Apple Media
1980 Lookout Drive, North Mankato, Minnesota 56003

Library of Congress Cataloging-in-Publication Data

Llewellyn, Claire.
Bones / by Claire Llewellyn.
p. cm. — (Starters)
Includes index.
ISBN 1-58340-562-3
1. Bones—Juvenile literature. [1. Bones.] I. Title. II. Series.

QP88.2.L585 2004
573.7'6—dc22   2003065918

9 8 7 6 5 4 3 2 1

The publishers would like to thank the following for allowing us to reproduce their
pictures in this book: Corbis; 8, 9 (right), 10 (right), 11 (top), 15 (top left, bottom
right), 16, 18, 20, 21, 22 / Ecoscene; 5 (bottom) / Hodder Wayland Picture Library;
title page, contents page, 4, 5 (top), 6, (right), 7, 9 (left), 10 (left), 11 (bottom), 12, 13,
14, 15 (top right and bottom left), 17, 23 / Martyn Chillmaid; 6 (left) / Mediscan; 19

Contents

Bony bodies

LONG bones, SHORT bones, FLAT bones, curvy bones—the bones in our bodies come in all shapes and sizes. Together, they make our skeleton, our body's bony frame.

frog

Many animals, and humans, have bony skeletons. We all belong to a group of animals called vertebrates.

hamster

4

crab

Crabs and slugs do not
have bones inside their bodies.
They belong to a group of
animals called invertebrates.

slug

Hard and strong

The skeleton is very important. This **strong**, bony frame supports the body and gives it its special shape.

A tent needs a framework to support it.

Your body needs one, too.

bones here
protect the brain
and eyes

bones here
protect the heart
and lungs

bones here protect
soft organs in the
lower body

Parts of the skeleton
protect organs, such as
the heart and lungs.
Animals depend on
these organs to survive.

A skeleton helps an animal to move. The bones are connected to muscles. When the muscles pull on the bones, the body starts to move.

The skeleton can move only where two bones meet. These parts of the skeleton are called joints.

An orangutan's shoulder joints allow its arms to swing freely.

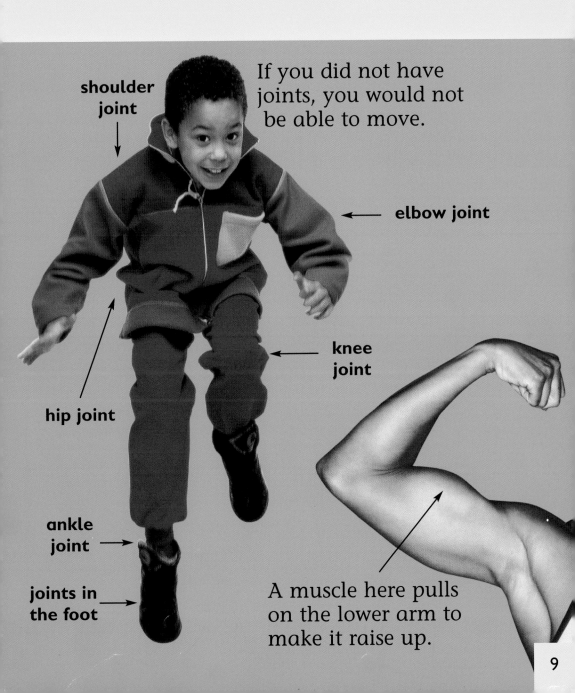

shoulder joint

If you did not have joints, you would not be able to move.

elbow joint

knee joint

hip joint

ankle joint

joints in the foot

A muscle here pulls on the lower arm to make it raise up.

Animal skeletons

An animal's skeleton can tell us a lot about its life. The size and shape of the bones can show us how it moved, where it lived, and what it ate.

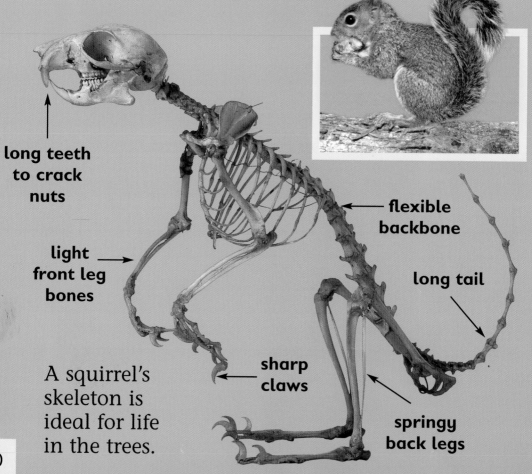

long teeth to crack nuts

light front leg bones

flexible backbone

long tail

sharp claws

springy back legs

A squirrel's skeleton is ideal for life in the trees.

This X-ray photo shows a snake's backbone. The small bones allow it to bend and curve as it swims, climbs, and burrows.

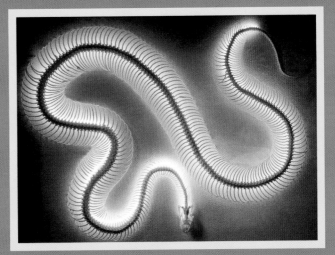

A fish's skeleton is perfect for moving through water.

stiff fins help fish turn and stay upright

strong tail fin

long, flexible backbone

The human skeleton

The human skeleton has more than 200 bones, and they all have a special name.

With 27 bones in our hand, we can grasp things such as pens.

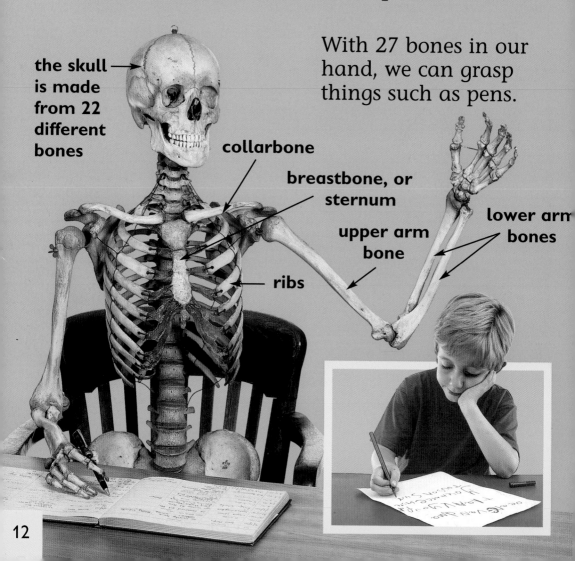

the skull is made from 22 different bones

collarbone

breastbone, or sternum

upper arm bone

lower arm bones

ribs

There are dozens of **tiny** bones in our hands and feet. These allow us to move in many different ways.

the spine is made of 33 small bones called vertebrae

pelvis

the thigh bone is the longest bone in the body

knee cap →

lower leg bones

foot bones

Looking at skulls

The skull protects the brain, eyes, ears, nose, and tongue. It is made up of 22 different bones, which join together when we are young.

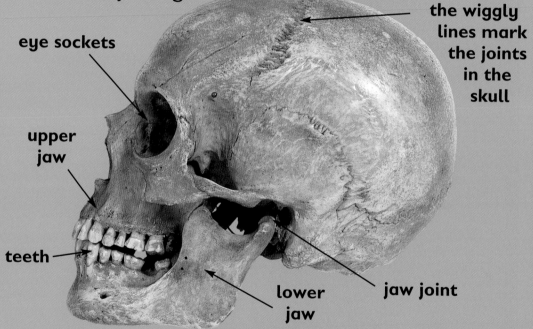

the wiggly lines mark the joints in the skull

eye sockets

upper jaw

teeth

lower jaw

jaw joint

The lower jaw is the skull's only moving part. The jaws help us to eat food. The **strong** teeth help to break the food down.

A deer's narrow skull lets it reach grass in almost every nook and cranny.

bony antlers

sharp front teeth cut grass

flat back teeth chew grass

A tiger's jaws give a powerful bite!

sharp teeth

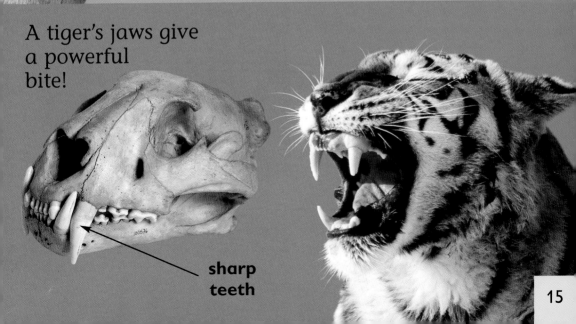

What is bone?

Bone is a strong, LIGHT material that is very durable, or long-lasting. Living bone is always changing and can replace itself with new bone.

A thigh bone is hard on the outside,

but the inside is light and spongy.

Bone contains calcium, which makes it very **STRONG**. Calcium is found in milk and cheese. So, if you want strong bones, drink milk!

Cheese, milk, and other healthy foods help to build strong bones.

Have you ever broken a bone? Broken bones can heal themselves by simply growing back together.

The two ends need to be held in place so that the bone grows straight and **strong**.

An X-ray shows doctors if a bone has broken. This X-ray shows a broken upper arm.

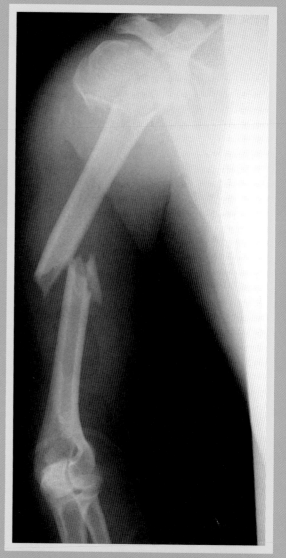

A broken leg takes about six to eight weeks to heal.

A plaster cast keeps it straight.

A bone sometimes breaks into many pieces. This X-ray shows how doctors can put it back together with metal screws and plates.

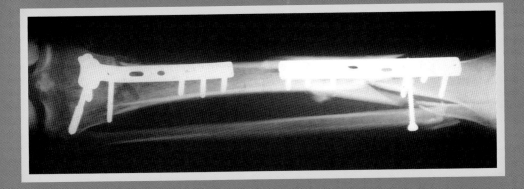

Growing and changing

When you were a baby, you had more than 300 tiny bones. Some of them were made of a rubbery material called cartilage.

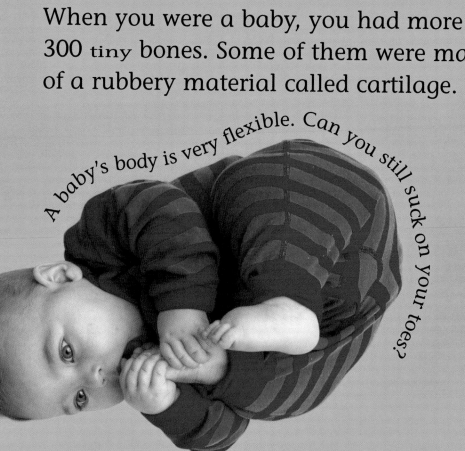

A baby's body is very flexible. Can you still suck on your toes?

Over the years, many of the bones join together, and the cartilage is replaced by harder, **stronger** bone.

As we grow
older, our bones
grow bigger.

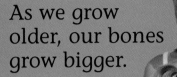

In older people, the bones
get THINNER, and joints
may begin to feel stiff.

Digging up bones

Scientists have dug up remains of animals that have been dead for millions of years.

Their bones didn't rot with the rest of their bodies. Instead, they were changed into stone. These stony remains are called fossils.

This fossil shows the skeleton of a fish.

skull

Fossils tell us about extinct animals that lived a long time ago. Who would have thought that old, dry bones could tell the story of life on Earth?

spine

ribs

Some of the biggest fossils are dinosaur bones. Scientists carefully put them together to build a dinosaur skeleton.

Glossary and index